My First Chinese Picture Books for Short Sentences Book 2

我的第一套中文短句绘本 2

Xiaolin Huang

To Cooper and Danna for being the pilot readers

First Published in Australia in 2017
This edition published in 2017
by Xiaolin Huang
ABN 60 520 297 573

Copyright Xiaolin Huang 2017
127 Cambridge Cres
Wyndham Vale
VIC 3024, Australia

http://fb.me/mfcpb

National Library of Australia Cataloguing-in-Publication entry

Creator: Huang, Xiaolin, author.

Title: My first Chinese picture books for short sentences. Book 2 : 我的第一套中文短句绘本 第二册 / Xiaolin Huang.

ISBN: 9780648102526 (paperback)

Target Audience: For preschool age

Subjects: Chinese characters--Juvenile literature
Chinese language--Writing--Juvenile literature
Chinese language--Juvenile literature
Picture books for children

我要喝水

我要喝果汁

我要吃西瓜

我要吃饼干

我要吃苹果

我要吃面包

我要玩手机

我要玩拼图

我要玩气球

爬山很好玩

自行车很好玩

滑滑梯很好玩

积木很好玩

葡萄很好吃

冰激淋很好吃

饼干很好吃

西瓜很好吃

电视很好看

天上的彩虹很好看

完

The End

本书常见字 试着认一认

Frequently Used Characters
Try to recognise and read

要	天	木
山	玩	车
水	我	瓜
好	吃	看
西	手	很

www.ingramcontent.com/pod-product-compliance
Lightning Source LLC
Chambersburg PA
CBHW061822290426
44110CB00027B/2952